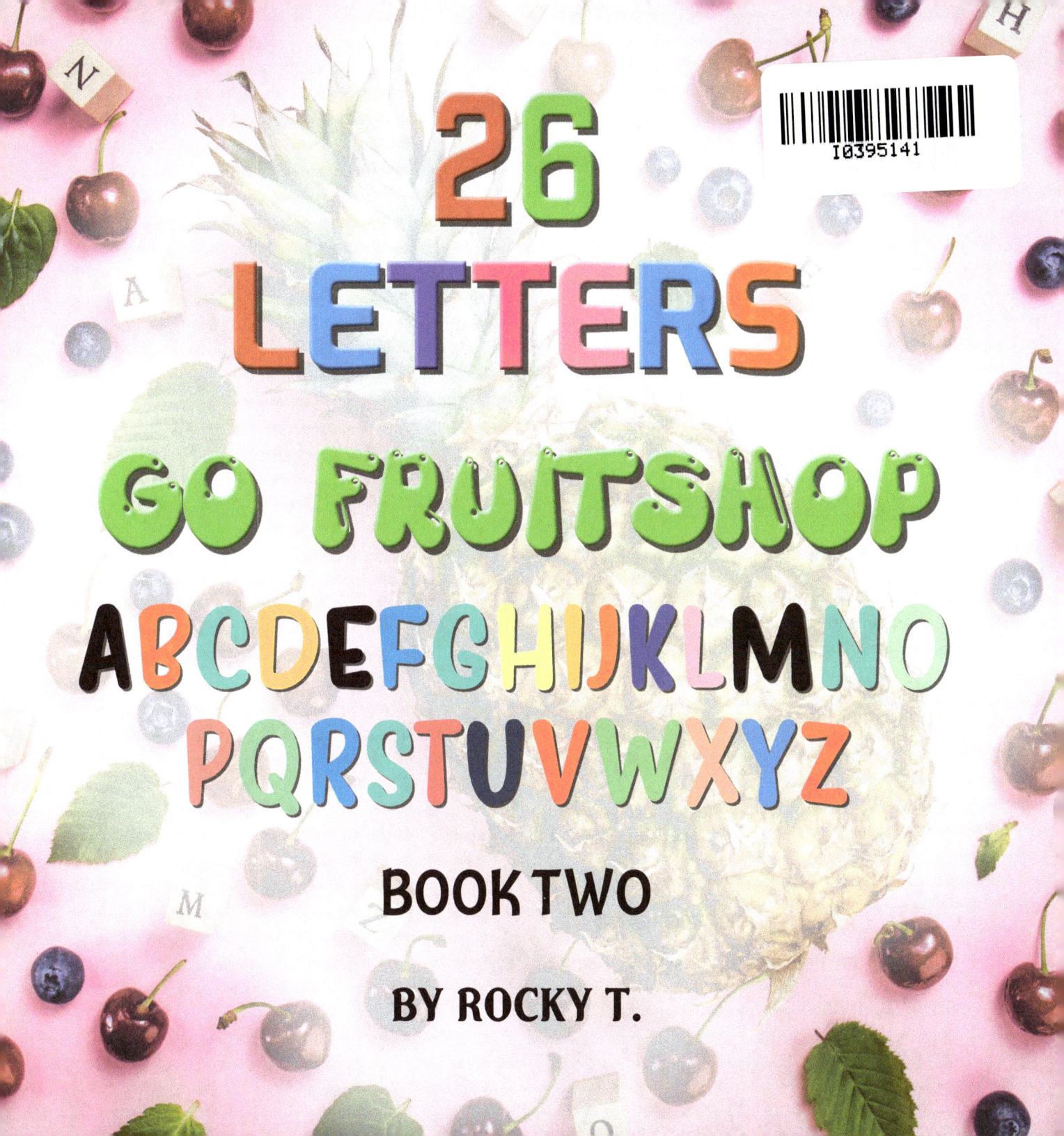

Copyright © 2023 Rocky Tropeano

All rights reserved.

No part of this book may be reproduced in any form or by any electronic or mechanical means including information storage and retrieval systems, without permission in writing from the Publisher.

Publishers:
Inspiring Publishers
P.O. Box 159
Calwell ACT 2905, Australia.
Email: inspiringpublishers@gmail.com

National Library of Australia Cataloguing-in-Publication entry

Author: **ROCKY TROPEANO**

Photos and Artwork: **ROCKY TROPEANO**

Title: **26 LETTERS: GO FRUITSHOP – Book 2**

ISBN: 978-1-922920-34-8 (Print)

Dedicated to all the hard working farmers and greengrocers I have had the privilage of meeting over the past 50 years.
Thank you - CHEERS from Rocky Tropeano.

A-is for apple = an apple a day keeps the dentist away-very healthy. Vitamin content = A+B1+B2+B6+C.

①

B-is for banana = bananas are a good source of energy so you can play-play-play at playtime. Vitamin content = A+Bl+B2+B6+C.

C-is for Carrot = carrots are good for ones eyesight the more the better. Vitamin content = beta caratone+ A+B1+B2+B6+C.

D-is for Dairy = dairy products contain calcium for bone strength and life wellbeing, drink milk.

E- is for Egg = a good source of protein for a healthy diet. Contains 75 calories + 7 grams of quality protein + 5 grams fat + 1.6 grams saturated fat and has disease fighting nutrients. Very good.

F-is for flower = flowers make you feel happy and brighten up the day for everyone. Usually gifts for loved ones or closest to you.

G-is for Grapefruit = like oranges are high in vitamin C+one grapefruit can give you 100% of your daily vitamin C.

H -is for Honeydew -has a lime tasting flesh -is very refreshing especially served cold. Vitamin content = Vit C+B6+B9+K.

I-is for Iceberg Lettuce = great in a salad or just plain healthy refreshing treat on its own. Vitamin content = high in minerals such as calcium-phosphorous-magnesium-potassium.

J-is for Jalapeno = jalapenos are often used in hamburgers or as pizza toppings CAUTION hot&spicey.

K-is for Kiwi Fruit = kiwi fruits have a cool lime flavour and are very refreshing anytime of day. Vitamin content = low in fat+cholesterol free+ sodium free+good source of potassium- high in vitamin C.

L-is for Lemon = lemons are good in mixed in tea to aid cold symptoms. Vitamin content = A+B1+B2+B6+C.

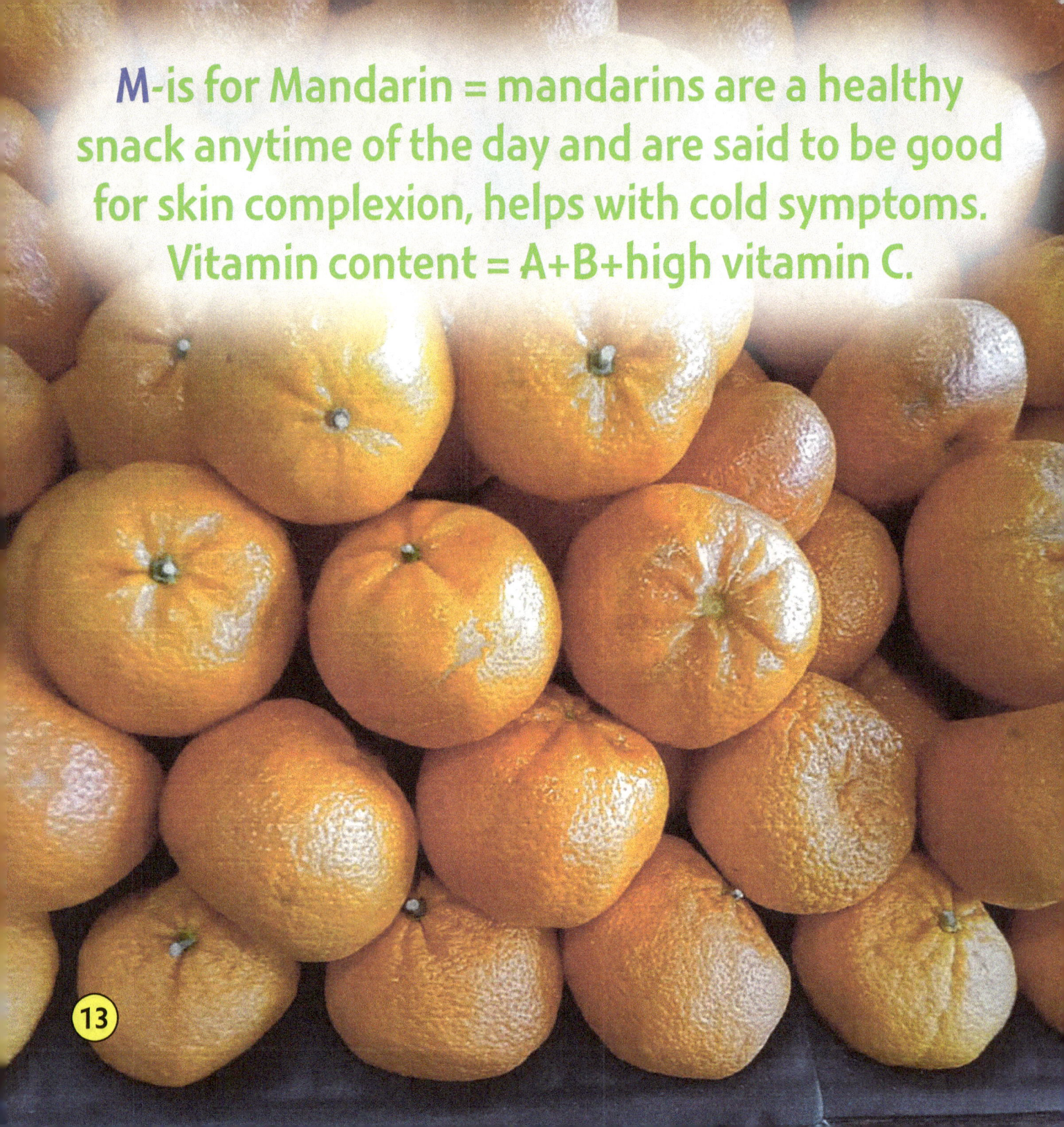

M-is for Mandarin = mandarins are a healthy snack anytime of the day and are said to be good for skin complexion, helps with cold symptoms. Vitamin content = A+B+high vitamin C.

N - is for Nuts = nuts are a good source of energy and help lower cholesterol in the body.

O- is for Orange = oranges are full of vitamin C to you strength and wellbeing very refreshing at anytime of day.
Vitamin content = A+B1+B2+B6+C.

P-is for Pear = pears are a tasty treat anytime of day-have all the goodness & freshness of fruit. Vitamin content = A+B1+B2+B6+C.

Q-is for Quinoa Seed = quinoa seeds are a healthy addition to a diet mixed into salads such as tabouli salad.

R- is for Radish = radish is a spiced addition to any salad or just good company on a cheese plater. Vitamin content = A+B1+B2+B6+C.

S-is for Strawberry = strawberries are a juicy tasty sweet anytime-great snack. Vitamin content = A+B1+B2+B6+C.

T- is for Tomato = tomatoes are filling on their own or in a salad-so nutritious. Vitamin content = A+B1+B2+B6+C.

U-is for Utensil = utensils are needed to crushslice-dice produce.

V-is for Vegetable = vegetables of any kind are tasty-filling-nutritious and healthy for growing bodies. Vitamin content = A+Bl+B2+B6+Vit C+Folate

W-is for Watermelon = watermelon is so refreshing anytime of the day. Vitamin content = A+Bl+B2+B6+vit C.

X-is for X-Ray = all eggs are checked by light for spots-only good eggs are packed for sale. Vitamin content = see Eggs.

Y - is for Yam = Yams are known as Sweet Potato in Australia, baked are best.
Vitamin content = fat free+cholesterol & sodium free high in vitamin A+C.

Z-is for Zucchini = zucchinis are a healthy source of energy fried or in a salad nutritious. Vitamin content = A+Bl+B2+B6+Vit C.

List of Fruit to EAT

Monday:
Tuesday:
Wednesday:
Thursday:
Friday:
Saturday:
Sunday:

List of Fruit to EAT

Monday:
Tuesday:
Wednesday:
Thursday:
Friday:
Saturday:
Sunday:

www.ingramcontent.com/pod-product-compliance
Lightning Source LLC
Chambersburg PA
CBHW081629100526
44590CB00021B/3659